Green Migraine

Also by Michael Dickman

Flies

The End of the West

50 American Plays
(with Matthew Dickman)

Michael
Dickman
Green
Migraine

COPPER CANYON PRESS
PORT TOWNSEND, WASHINGTON

Printed in the United States of America

Cover art: Photo by Cindy August

Copper Canyon Press is in residence at Fort Worden State Park in Port Townsend, Washington, under the auspices of Centrum. Centrum is a gathering place for artists and creative thinkers from around the world, students of all ages and backgrounds, and audiences seeking extraordinary cultural enrichment.

LIBRARY OF CONGRESS CATALOGING-IN-PUBLICATION DATA

Dickman, Michael, 1975–
  [Poems. Selections]
  Green migraine : poems / Michael Dickman.
      pages ; cm
  ISBN 978-1-55659-451-9 (pb : alk. paper)
  I. Title.

PS3604.I299A6 2015
811'.6—dc23

2015023777
98765432 FIRST PRINTING

COPPER CANYON PRESS
Post Office Box 271
Port Townsend, Washington 98368
www.coppercanyonpress.org

Acknowledgments

Grateful acknowledgment is due to the editors of *The Believer, Brick, Granta, jubilat, The New Yorker, Paperbag, Ploughshares,* and *Poetry.*

The migraine poems were first collected into a chapbook called *Auras* and published by Ibidem.

Special thanks to my friends and colleagues at the Lewis Center for the Arts at Princeton University, for much-appreciated support.

for *August*

Contents

Green Migraine

Bee Sting

Crying in the cosmos that doesn't sound like you

Crying in our arms
in the cosmos in our
arms

Missile static and afterburn in the petals

Your yellow-
and-black stingers

A child's drawing

Some riddle from before we were born that sounds like a river and spreads on
        toast

And floats
from flower to
flower

The first needle

The honey in the pot

———

I've always wanted
to wake up surrounded by
buzz and fuzz

My head lifted by a furry crown set sailing into the late drone afternoon
 drifting at the speed of sound

My mouth full of strange sunlight

Killer bumble honey
in the brain

Dusting the earth

Sail on
Sail on
Sail on

I've always wanted
to bump the stamen and start
the universe swaying

Those ten thousand wings you hear coming for you are yours my little
      honeybee

Burning in place
in space

Pinprick in the epileptic air

Swept up from corners
and wrapped in
banana leaves

Are you hungry?

Alive in the center of the room
Alive in flowers

Your white shoulders and white rump

Invisible death's-head
turning on and off
in the dark

Dog Vertigo

Some teeth down there
some hair and gray
gums

Some grass and dirt
down there some gristle
and whimpers

All stupid grinning death running around the yard making a little child cry
   with each busted grass blade

I had a dog
I had three dogs
I sit and stay

They did not disappear into
the trees one day

Their brains were not broken coral on the street

They were meat

———

Some leash
down there some shit
and tennis balls

I had a dog
I had three dogs
I sit and beg

Their brains were not broken coral on the street

They were not meat
one day they did not disappear
into the trees

All stupid grinning death running around the yard making a little child cry
        with each busted grass blade

Some whimpers
down there some nipples
and pink tum-tums

———

Some biting tails
down there some sunlight
and long nails

Some fleas dug up some mange and gray tongues

I had a dog
They were meat
I had three dogs

They did not disappear into the streets
They did not tree

Some haunch skid
and drag down there some
mouths one day

They did not smell like baby's breath

All stupid grinning death running around the yard making a little child cry
       with each busted grass blade

Some grass and dirt
down there some teeth and
ruined carpets

I had a dog
I had three dogs
I fucked fleas

All stupid grinning death running around the yard making a little child cry
        with each busted grass blade

Some eyelashes
down there some eating grass
and mange some
baby's breath

One day their brains were not broken
coral on the street

They did not disappear into the trees

Some sit and stay
down there some meat
and sunlight

Their brains were not
broken coral on the street they
did not disappear into
the trees

They did not fuck fleas

All stupid grinning death running around the yard making a little child cry
        with each busted grass blade

Some bones and baby's breath down there
some bark and seizures

Distant watery eyes

One day I had a dog

I had three dogs

White Migraine

Every color
there ever was
is white

It peels the skin back from the roof of your mouth in metal petals that taste
       like snow

The roof of the world

My fingernails
in a pile

The moon flushed down a toilet

Everything
I ever wanted glows
in the moonlight

What do you want?

I want to be sick and white and cough up

lilies of the valley

The Matterhorn
in my shoulders ruptures
in the toilet

My mouth walks down a hallway in a hospital

Clouds
of bone and cum
in the brainpan

White caviar gets scooped out from the back of my eyeballs with delicate spoons

The mother-of-pearl spoons are tuned razor sharp

And sing
from an iceberg
in the ice cream

It turns out white can make the world

absolutely clean

On all fours
the universal position
of love is white

An oyster shell turned over on a bed of ice is an oyster shell turned over on a
       bed of lice

The white tongues
speaking to me now speak
in white tongues

Are you loved?
Are you loved?
Are you loved?

I sit beneath the avalanche and wait

My master
plan

is happiness

Red Migraine

Redbreast kills
and kills itself against
the window

Sooner or later the blood in the breast will break the window into hundreds of
pieces you can swallow whole

Keep swallowing!

Redbreast
loves you or wants you
to remember the love

So it makes you puke into the toilet blind

I was blinded by love

And drowned
in an empty bathtub
spitting up birdshit

Covered in red feathers

Sometimes redbreast likes anting with lit cigarettes safety pins paper cuts God
    that feels good

It wraps everything
in pretty pink gauze the color
of fake sunset

A pink soul

It wants to get naked and it wants it to hurt

Red teeth
Red toes
Open mouths

Who keeps pressing my head into the sidewalk
inside the bathroom

Who keeps the lights on

Who dissolves on my tongue

Who flies from my finger

———

Redbreast sits inside
behind your left eye
behind your right and cleans
its babies with
its beak

Scrubs its babies clean

Shakes its tail feathers to scour the floor behind your forehead and scours the
   floor red

My brain is a cutter

My initials are beats per second

Scrubbed down to zero
by the rubies
in the halo

I whispered your name into the red air

and you answered

Butterflies

Sketchy
through a hole in the butterfly day
an orange-and-yellow
slipstream

Better than birds

Hanging laundry by remote control

Drinking Coca-Cola
and imitating roses in the pink
suburbs

There is no way to guess which way they'll go just scraps of air and then
      nothing at all like AM radio

Careful with each other

Hands glued together with Elmer's

Pinned
to brown particleboard

Deer Crossing

You can't shove
your mind into their little
mean hooves no matter
what you do

Running at night surrounded by hair ticks and twin brothers

On sucked pavement

Broken dishes

If I flick my tail will you flick your tail and everyone flicks their tail before the
        air resettles our ears

A bestiary
hangs from the roof
of my mouth

Eating grass in pharmaceutical fields

Head down
in the sicko green

Curves through
the deer crossing and slow
down for children

A wet ribbon

Sometimes pinballs
for eyes tongue in a drain
and a crossed-out
stomach

Soft as butter

Your legs are soft as butter

Unbroken necks twitch followed by one hundred backsides disappearing into
        white clouds and canal trash

Streaming through broken apples

Apple cider

A girdle full of fruit

Nothing but buttercups
here and one or two mamas
and papas

Licking themselves into a batter

Night noses
brown river and white
bellies
suitcases for flies
maggot bath and
shit slick

It's either spring or it's not

Crossing in the morning light without thinking there's no way around it we
sound like the rain

Tin cans

Striking sparks in high-heel shoes

Yellow Migraine

Daffodils shimmy
in the dilated onion grass
their hearts out

Shelovesme Shelovesmenot

Smeared
against the sidewalk

Urine left in the toilet all day simmers under halogens

Listening
to someone else breathe
listening to static cling

Time to wipe down the refrigerator with a handful of ibuprofen and a bandanna
        soaked in tonic water

Butter-butter
Black lemons
Pine-Sol

Daffodils shimmy
in the dilated onion grass
their asses off

Other yellow flowers I don't see you yet

Noon
tears down the street
a terrible kid
on a brand-new

Now I remember the faces of tulips

Speechless

Yellow peaches
sweat inside brown
paper bags

Press your forehead against the pit in the perfect peach and everything will stop
       moving how about that?

———

Daffodils shimmy
in the dilated onion grass
their eyes closed

Close your eyes I close my eyes

Families of worms work their yellow way up through clouds in the mustard air

Slams into the yard

Pollen
lies down on everything
it just lies down
sun the color of
photosynthesis and
that's fine

Birds bark inside houses

Yellow fingers work the yellow spine

Frog Labor

Frogs make a sound
they make a sound
in the round

Crickets combing their teeth and hedge trimmers don't make the same
        heartbeat in a puddle

Nothing does

Perfect small
glass balls wiggle and jiggle
like gelatin and smell
like the sun

You can't pop them
between your fingers because
they won't pop

A rain shower

You roll them on your tongue

———

Everyone wants
to be a mama here
you can be a mama
here too

If you want to

Eggs beaten into stiff white peaks that can see

Toes somehow on their way

Bones straight up
from the Day-Glo
tar pits

Hi Mama!

A dozen large white inside the head of every frog like a box of lightbulbs in a
        plastic bag

Or a thumbnail of apple juice

Or green mousse

It's loud down
there and getting louder
down there

Frog eggs get bigger and bigger until they are a full moon and don't fit anywhere

They don't fit inside a washing machine

They don't fit in your pocket

Kicky legs
and slippery fingers

Green sponges
left inside a heart transplant
have the hiccups

We wait and wait to hear
our names

Come out come out wherever you are

Mouse Hunt

Your little eyes
brake lights and gray fur
scrunched up beneath
the house

Your huge balls and small hands

Your see-through babies still alive in the dirt blinking those blind fruit jellies
       still alive

Your frozen nose
searching for your brothers
and sisters

I couldn't hit you with a hammer

That little hiss you make
Puffball

Oh look

You have a mother

Your whiskers in a storm

Your pleasure center radio antennae checking the latest score

Bumblebee marbles of shit

Your ears folded over like paper airplanes covered in birch bark flying through
      heavy fog

Your thoughts somewhere else
altogether now

Singing late into the night
in the kitchen
under the humped
linoleum

Chasing the cat through the Comet

Your legs ride
a bicycle in your sleep
until you stop

———

Your family curled
in a cupboard eating themselves
in circles

Your dreams rolled up inside the paper towels

Perfect teeth
silver fillings and expensive
new crowns

Your tumors dancing beneath the inverted black bowl of your crushed
    mulberry skull

Dancing like jugs of milk

Lighting the way between the bedroom and bath

Your pure pink
Pepto-Bismol on the bottoms
of your feet

Last thing every night before bed

From the Canal

for Paul Muldoon

Small fistfuls
of green lights hang
from your every
word

An alphabet I can't read

Illiterate
in sunlight

The box turtles stack up one on top of the other like newly minted money
        balanced above the water

I am so happy
I would like to take some drugs
some cherry blossoms

Dogwoods

I would like to chop down my shoulders into flowers

A spray of flowers

Someone breathes
on a dead deer
and its eyelashes
panic

High beams
in the rubber trees

Rain floods eyeholes that see everything reflected back from skidding black
    macadam

Someone cut your feet off

Someone moved your leg across the street

Someone whistled

Giving birth
you give birth to steam
and maggots

Strange new butterflies

A blue heron looks back one million years from the muddy bank and is ready
        for liftoff

It lifts off
through a shower curtain
of dragonflies and
pollen

It wants to be alone
It wants to stand on one leg forever

And be a ballerina
in curved space and
a black crown

Everything is so still that I can't breathe

The joggers pound the dirt and will never die

Fish asleep on the bottom

Insects screaming in the trees

Fox buckled
the color of oatmeal
a small potato bug
with teeth

Singing a song when no one is looking not your mother not your father
hardwired to square bales of hay

Gray fox moving in fields and dead in fields
one or the other
you choose

You choose with your teeth what to sing

Disappearing into blank

A dried-out wasps' nest in your hair

A rope full of knots
rubble for eyes
and broken-up concrete

———

Gnats rise as one
white feathered lung
and breathe

They have nowhere to go

Maybe they want to build a little city
inside my chest

Floor after floor
of air conditioning
and glass

Why do I keep waiting for something to change when I know that nothing will
      change?

Light crumples
against the hammered brass
heads of frogs

Two boys carry a snake between them like a live extension cord

Green Migraine

Some dragonflies
down there some static
and dirty diapers

I'll never
get back to sleep this way

Dandelion teeth drop from a spring sky and skitter the surface of a pond and
      the perfectly still grass

Shake
shake
shake it but don't
break break break it

I can almost get it with these tweezers

Chlorine in the cupola

Feedback
out of ferns

The eyes in frogs
like eggs all burst at the same time
from eggshells

Green sky
Green sky
Green sky

Some moss
up there some clouds
getting sick

See those hummingbirds?

I painted those with a silver-tipped paintbrush and an unopened bottle of mint
      cream amitriptyline

The peas in the pod cry out and then roll to the floor

In flames

The rind on the watermelon smiles

Tree ants melt
in my mouth and leaves
end in algae

Grasshoppers vibrate

The night was green the morning was green and now it's late afternoon inside
a lawn mower

Some kids in there
some chlorophyll and
sunburn

It doesn't hurt so much with the blinds shut

It doesn't hurt
when a leaf falls
to the ground

It's the sound

The grass in the yard stands straight up

Butterflies

Sonic drag
and television snow
in the rhododendrons

White scales smudge the windows

Fluttery

It's all
just description

A wall of butterflies falls apart in the middle of the air or flies back together
        again like drywall

Their eyes are spackled

All together in a pile above the grass they look fluorescent

Children
coming home from school at noon

Their legs go tick-tick

Someone changes the channel inside a cocoon

Black Migraine

The saints come marching in
through a hole
in the sky

Do you remember me?

I remember
you

Black hole
Black saints

The killed gold hems of their skirts brush gently against my eyelids is what it
        feels like not what it is

Their shoes are beautiful

They sit at the right hand of the brain stem
and shake
and shake

the retard maypole

Music comes and goes
through the dead
speakers

Black dials

They twist
like telephone wire

A line of ants running from an outlet in the black oak to the back of my throat
        is always plugged in

Hello hello
Are you there?
I am here

I have passed out in the yard

The ants
look just like cuff links
and carry small black trumpets

Someone keeps ripping the stitches out and then sewing them up again are they
	using their teeth

Every sound
shovels my forehead
into the ground

Tamps it down

Sudden girls
playing hopscotch
on the blacktop
in the sun

I thought I was going to puke with you in paradise forever

Oh I want to be in that number

Bright
laces and black
bubblegum

A Cloudless Sky

A cloudless sky and I'm back
an ice-cold sky-blue rag
for my eyes

Nobody move I said
between every stutter of light
and someone is cutting
yellow grass a block away

A cloudless sky is
wiped clean

Music that's left over and hangs on everything sounds like it could use some
more gasoline

Nobody gets hurt

Grass disappears behind the blinds

Was that really a lawn mower or
no was it bees

A cloudless sky shuts
the door behind me softly so
softly like cotton soaked
in alcohol

I start at the tips of my toes

Moving up
through a pile of blue
pine needles

Moving down

This part won't hurt a bit it's just children or birds exploding in a game you
can't see

A cloudless sky
can see

Birds corkscrew

Jump ropes scrape the sidewalk

A cloudless sky asleep

will wake to the sound of the AC

and turn and fall again

in love with a glass of water

and a green pill

I used to sleep in sheets now I sleep in mint jelly

I wish there were an opposite shore

you could swim

from one end to the other of

without a wave

Thunderheads piling up across the bedroom are something I can feel beneath
        my fingernails

A cloudless sky pares its nails with scissors

in the shape of a bird

The tide goes out but the air stays on

A cloudless sky won't cry into its pillow like a toilet flushed over and over no
     eyes anymore just ice cubes

Who is cutting
someone else in half?

I can hear sunlight
I can hear grass
I can hear my hair

Let the ice from the ice tray shine on me

I used to live
in a house now I live
in a cloudless sky

One cloud is gone

One cloud is not moving a muscle

I don't move a muscle

One cloud is a good little boy

Foxtrot

Dear fox where have you been?

Dead on the dance floor
in the middle of
a field

Your natural weave frozen to the dirt

Your face frozen
cheek to cheek and
palm to palm

I want my arms
around you your red hair
bleached blue

Ants walk right through your rib cage

What ate your insides out

Out-all-night music whistles through a feather finish and your new permanent
    smile

I do a feather hover
above your broken
collar

Your legs cross quietly at the ankle
Your teeth floss a tuft of grass
Everything is just one color

Dead fox
good morning

I can't smell hay
when it's this cold out I can't
smell farms

I can't hear hot renditions of Cake Walking Babies from Home or Ain't She
        Sweet and look at you

You must be tired

Your hands closed your eyes missing

———

A quickstep won't save you now foxtrot or reverse turn your spine back into a
    xylophone

Fast
Fast
Slow
Slow

You look like you've been doing yoga in a freezer bag

Hunger pose
between the Birds Eye
and Häagen-Dazs

Your teeth sparkle
I just have time to rent a tuxedo

Inside your chest
falls one flake of snow

Outside your chest it gets darker earlier

Where We Live

for John Guare

I used to live
in a mother now I live
in a sunflower

Blinded by the silverware

Blinded by the Frigidaire

I sit on a sidewalk
in the sunflower and its yellow
downpour

The light of the world
beads up on one perfect
green leaf

It scribbles its name on every living thing then erases it so what's left is more of
     a whisper than a mother

Here it's spring

Over and over and over again

———

I used to live
in a cloud now I live
in a crow

It's tiny and crippled in there but I can find my way to the bathroom in the
dark if I need to

All the windows
in the crow are left open
and let the clouds in

Back in

They float past my bed and have nothing to say

Hello it's nice to meet you!

On a telephone pole
dinosaur toes rock
back and forth

Back and forth

———

I used to live
in a mouse now I live
in a dog

Chasing butterflies into the ground

All the little mouse bones
piled up in a corner of
the dog

Gray cotton
candy blows around
inside us

Allergic to cheese

Allergic to chocolate

The dog runs me around the chain-link in circles that get wider and wider until
     I'm eating grass in a hole

Rat grass inside the oat grass

I used to live
in a tree now I live
in a king

He waves his arms in front and endless migrations of birds disappear into his
        coat

I like to sit up inside
his crown eating sandwiches
and watching TV

Hills shake in the distance when he shuffles his feet
Floods when he snaps his fingers

I bow inside his brow and the afternoon stretches out

Orders more sandwiches

Sells the slaves
sets the slaves free
sells the slaves

Butterflies

Upside-down overhead projectors from brown grade school

We say your name and we clap for you

Our small small
bodies and our big big
heads

Eyes on everything

They look like thinking
Mud-puddling in mud
or alcohol

I lie on my back with my feet in the air

An egg stuck on a leaf a hundred eggs
A chandelier

The stereo pumped into the backyard and the patio furniture left out it just
        makes everything feel better

Take one by mouth every hour

John Clare

Now I remember
I wanted to talk to you
between your Selected Poems
and the punk rock music
playing on the radio

Between the blue irises and the Mexican lawn service

The skaters and the dragonflies

Do you know what it's like here?

Scared beneath trees
the spotlight on the one rose
is the one spotlight

The sun keeps going

Tell me something between the yellowhammers and the leaf blowers

Between a worm getting pulled out of the dirt into the sky and a worm
      progging the dark

———

Children play in the past
in pastures and now I remember
7-Eleven parking lots
skateboarding through
black fields

Cows move through the fields to the fence and won't move again

Cows move
through the parking lot
toward a bike rack
in the heather

Black tongues
park out front and idle their engines

Daisies chain and unchain

In the morning someone hoses down the hot concrete and insects crawl
through your name

The dogs are shy and snap

chew through chain link

each other and now I remember fur

and won't let go or be beaten

to death by kids

Let the fur fly!

The boys ollie over the dogs

in their dreams

In dreams

some of the boys

kiss them on the mouth

Their mouths are clean and their noses are pink

All the dogs I grew up with are gone

They were someone's sweethearts shitting on the sidewalk in the sun

Flowers call you
on the telephone and the rain
passes you notes
none of us will ever read
now I remember every line
pistils texting
from the ground cover

Peonies drip onto the ground
making long-distance calls
person to person

The car alarms sound like roses

There are roses peonies and giant white papery things the size of your face
      and ferns

Ferns ferns ferns

The loves of my life

———

Birds are never lonely next to you

in neighborhoods

and wings clear the air

and are gone

into holes or headaches

Now I remember

There are holes all around

Holes in children

Holes in trees

Holes in the water and in the teeth of small animals if you can see that and can
you see that

And wasps

eating entire families of deer

Here

I wanted to show you

Lullaby

Something shifts
a little to the left during takeoff
and I'm gone

Hello trees

Hospital parking lot hello again hello

The light arrived from light-years away and hit the ground exactly thirty
       seconds later than yesterday

Splitting everything in half

My pregnant wife one two my brain and how can you be more than one thing

But I am!

Trees
Empty parking spaces
Machines I
don't understand

The water here breaks and breaks

Water breaks
over my sneaks and now
I remember rain

I grew up in rain

Rain
Rain
Blood in little blood puddles

Well we are blood people

The afterbirth sloshed into a blue bucket smelled like finger paint

All three of us stayed on earth in ruined underwear and tubes going in and the
      delivery room floated

He was huge
not in love yet purple brown
purple red and looked around and was not a baby toy

He was a WOLFBOY

What howls
all day in the next room
and sleeps and sleeps

A dozen pink carnations
opening all at once
from the exact center of the known universe

Petals
falling to the floor
get things started

In central New Jersey
the room spins once and
you're here

Asleep in a car seat on the living room floor

The blood left back at the hospital the mud washed off and all that blue animal
        hair down the drain

Animals are here
and night and day and noises
are here and wolves
and birds

Trees are here and John Clare is here
Hello John

Your forehead furred your fingers fronds

Your throat cheeping

Look look we said and pointed out the window at the moon the moon your
      eyes iced-over pinpoints

Your unbelievable feet

Whales are here and pillows and poems
Your teeth are hiding

Little ears

Do you want to see those birds?

Birds talk and try
to find each other and don't
see you yet

I said look it's a tree

I said look it's a glass of milk

When your head crowned the midwife said look it's a head she was right I
        didn't touch you yet

Milk floats through the leaves

I think every bird tweetweetwee is a baby bird tawee tawee

Honeybees asleep
asleep beneath the snow
can't hear you

Little hands

We'll roll them over

We'll wake them up

Wake up
Wake up
It's time to get up

Your blood flickers beneath the muddy surface of a cup of coffee you are not a
        little bird I don't chew up your food

Your flat animal breathing
hard all night

The house breathing

Some fur still on you we haven't rubbed off yet

Some oil we need to lick

A floodlight in a crib
A glass of milk asleep

You are so new
you could be gone tomorrow
and no one would know what to do

Black-bellied
whistling ducks are here
and know what to do

Common loons are here and pileated woodpeckers cattle egrets and great blue
herons have stepped carefully into the water

Turkey vultures
are here and black
vultures

A red-shouldered
A broad-winged
A rough-legged hawk is here

Ploots plovers and oystercatchers and house wrens are here

Winter wrens in winter

and chickadees all the way from Carolina

here to see you

All the way
from endless maple trees
and maple leaves
to see you

I was a baby once now you're a baby

This morning you do not have
a tail or extra fingers you do not
have any twins

A small pink knot

A pool of jelly on the top of your head that breathes when you breathe a little
        frog sac I can see through

Two eyes

You do not have extra legs or fins you do not have feathers

All around the kitchen

Cock-a-doodle-doodle-do

A sweet gum tree is here

black gum and black

maples

Bloodgood and cherries are here

Something sings

in the slippery elm and

I'm gone

The pin oak is here and willow oak the willow oak and the shadblow

serviceberry is here for you to crawl beneath

Cock-a-doodle-doodle-do

A flowering

dogwood is here it doesn't

say anything

White ash or green ash you can hardly tell the difference

The sidewalks are a mess

Your eyes are here
straight from your big animal mama
your fingernails are here and
now look some teeth

Walking down the sidewalk toward me

Wobbly

Not a jellyfish

Your two hands are here two legs your brain is here a small snowy owl or a
        stuffed blue whale made out of a pair of pants

Your perfectly drawn star anus

Your unperturbed penis

Your straw hair
from a children's book
keeps growing

Your knees above the pavement are here one small explosion after another

A tiger in a crown
is here and says Hello
Hello

A car full of dogs has nowhere to go

Where will they live?

A moon on every page and a great horned owl a barred owl is here short-eared
long-eared a screech owl is here

Entrails in the snow

A bear in your bed

A boy in a quart of milk
is here a boy who can't
find his dragon

A snake dog is here an elephant
an alligator is here and a hippo a rhino
and a deathless lion

Everyone lives in a tree

I live with you and your mama
inside a little house and a backyard
full of black squirrels
and I'm here

Up trees and down trees in crazy homing device zigzag that only they can
        follow and I'm here

Leaves chatter outside the window

I live with you and your mama in the leaves

Two trees
Hearts and hands
Nibble-nibble

I live with you and your mama in the morning
going ooie ooie ooie
dee dee dee doh

The black squirrels lick each other clean

Your damp head
a clump of pudgy ferns
is here

Your voice that chelps chickers and chitters
from your crib
and down the stairs
is here

You scrawl across the living room floor

You sawn and shool

Your tongue
is here a small fish
is here a struttle

You used to do your thing in the dark growing fingernails and eyeballs now
    your mouth is here mizled in the totter grass

Your baby fat left behind in the toddler grass

What arrived from light-years away is here already spinning in the kitchen
        practicing his ABCs

Blood all over the floor and then story time

Just like that

I don't care
about the names of trees
I don't care about flowers

Your mama is here a miracle in blue jeans
Your mama is here

You are asleep

Something shifts
a little to the left during takeoff
and I'm gone

Hello AUGUST

Little boy hello again hello

About the Author

Michael Dickman was born and raised in Portland, Oregon.

Lannan Literary Selections

For two decades Lannan Foundation has supported the publication and distribution of exceptional literary works. Copper Canyon Press gratefully acknowledges their support.

LANNAN LITERARY SELECTIONS 2015

Michael Dickman, *Green Migraine*

Deborah Landau, *The Uses of the Body*

Camille Rankine, *Incorrect Merciful Impulses*

Richard Siken, *War of the Foxes*

Frank Stanford, *What About This: Collected Poems of Frank Stanford*

RECENT LANNAN LITERARY SELECTIONS FROM COPPER CANYON PRESS

James Arthur, *Charms Against Lightning*

Mark Bibbins, *They Don't Kill You Because They're Hungry, They Kill You Because They're Full*

Malachi Black, *Storm Toward Morning*

Marianne Boruch, *Cadaver, Speak*

Jericho Brown, *The New Testament*

Olena Kalytiak Davis, *The Poem She Didn't Write and Other Poems*

Natalie Diaz, *When My Brother Was an Aztec*

Matthew Dickman and Michael Dickman, *50 American Plays*

Kerry James Evans, *Bangalore*

Tung-Hui Hu, *Greenhouses, Lighthouses*

Deborah Landau, *The Last Usable Hour*

Sarah Lindsay, *Debt to the Bone-Eating Snotflower*

Michael McGriff, *Home Burial*

Valzhyna Mort, *Collected Body*

Lisa Olstein, *Little Stranger*

Roger Reeves, *King Me*

Ed Skoog, *Rough Day*

For a complete list of Lannan Literary Selections from Copper Canyon Press, please visit Partners on our website: www.coppercanyonpress.org

Poetry is vital to language and living. Since 1972, Copper Canyon Press has published extraordinary poetry from around the world to engage the imaginations and intellects of readers, writers, booksellers, librarians, teachers, students, and donors.

WE ARE GRATEFUL FOR THE MAJOR SUPPORT PROVIDED BY:

THE PAUL G. ALLEN FAMILY FOUNDATION

Anonymous

John Branch

Diana Broze

Beroz Ferrell & The Point, LLC

Janet and Les Cox

Mimi Gardner Gates

Linda Gerrard and Walter Parsons

Gull Industries, Inc.
on behalf of William and
Ruth True

Mark Hamilton and Suzie Rapp

Carolyn and Robert Hedin

Steven Myron Holl

Lakeside Industries, Inc.
on behalf of Jeanne Marie Lee

Maureen Lee and Mark Busto

Brice Marden

Ellie Mathews and Carl Youngmann
as The North Press

H. Stewart Parker

Penny and Jerry Peabody

John Phillips and Anne O'Donnell

Joseph C. Roberts

Cynthia Lovelace Sears and
Frank Buxton

The Seattle Foundation

Kim and Jeff Seely

David and Catherine Eaton Skinner

Dan Waggoner

C.D. Wright and Forrest Gander

Charles and Barbara Wright

The dedicated interns and faithful volunteers of Copper Canyon Press

TO LEARN MORE ABOUT UNDERWRITING COPPER CANYON PRESS TITLES, PLEASE CALL 360-385-4925 EXT. 103

The Chinese character for poetry is made up of two parts:
"word" and "temple." It also serves as pressmark for
Copper Canyon Press.

The poems are set in Sabon. Headings are set in Classic Grotesque.
Printed on archival-quality paper.
Book design and composition by Phil Kovacevich.